"I'm Not a Monster!"

Written by
Jill Atkins

I'm a **water bear**. Some people call me a **moss piglet**.

Can you count how many legs I have? I can live almost anywhere, from the tops of mountains to the bottom of the deep sea.

I may look rather frightening, but I'm not a monster.

I'm very, very small, so you can hardly spot me without a microscope!

I was chosen to go on a special mission … into space.
I stayed alive because I can survive without air in almost any temperature.

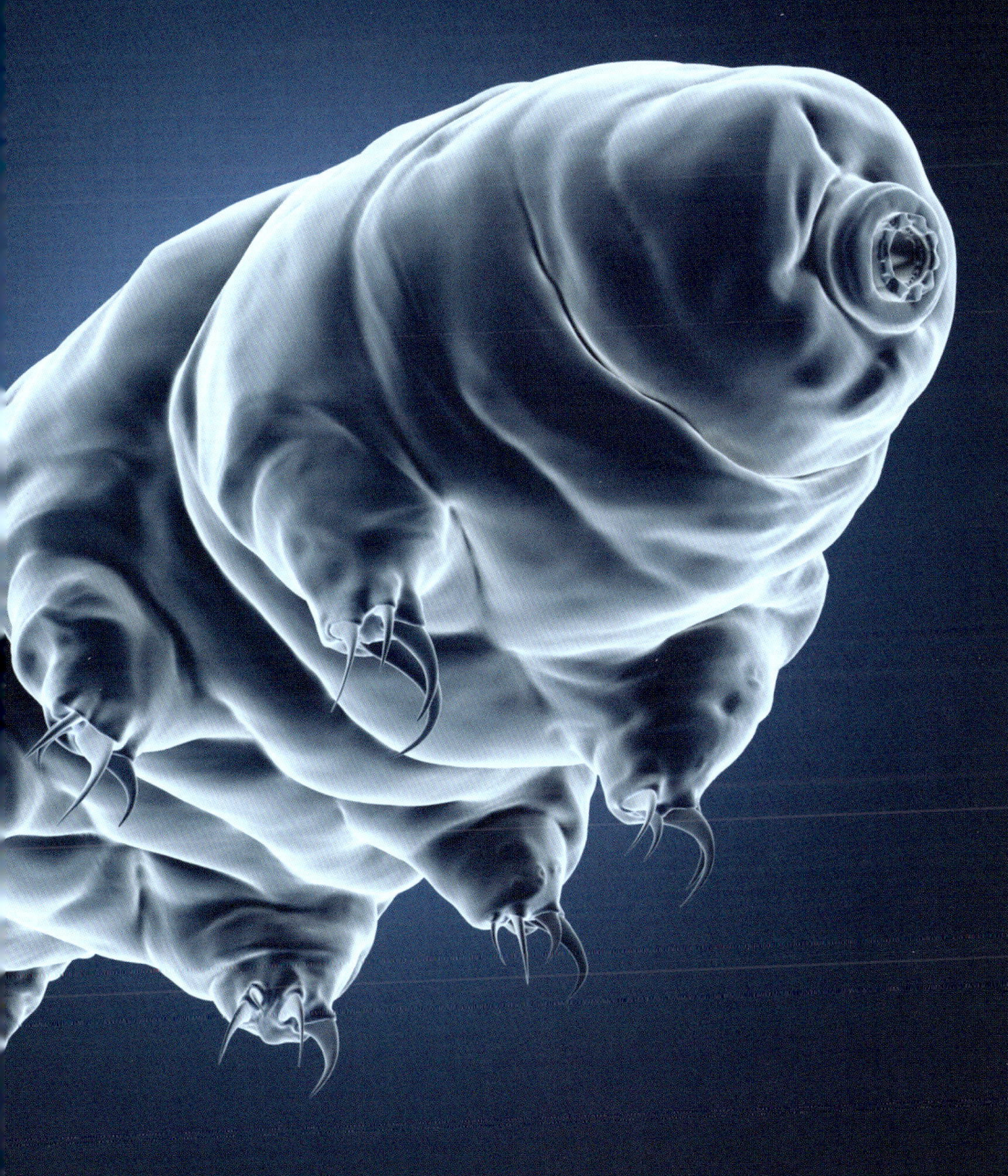

I'm a **duck-billed platypus**. I'm a mammal, but I lay eggs, which is very unusual. I've got a beak like a duck, a body like an otter and a tail like a beaver.

Some of us have venom, like a snake. Our venom can kill small animals.

But I'm not a monster.

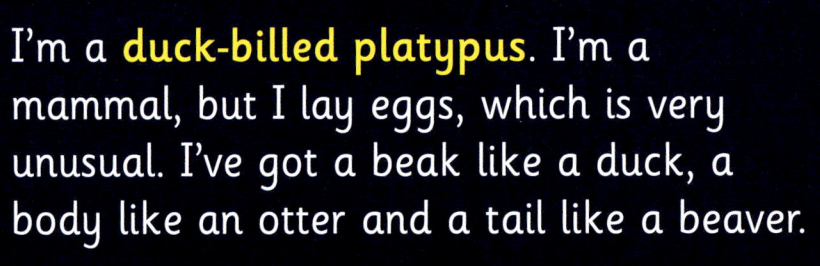

I'm a brilliant swimmer and spend half my time under water, searching for food.

Sadly, my habitat is fast disappearing and we now face extinction.

I'm a **star-nosed mole**. People think my nose looks ugly. They might say it looks like a bunch of little fingers, sticking out of my face.

But I'm not a monster.

They're not fingers – they're feelers, and they're special.

I need them because I'm totally blind. My feelers can detect worms and insects in the earth, so I can eat.

I'm a **thorny lizard**. I inhabit dry rocky places and I'm covered in scales and sharp spikes. Do you think I look like a dragon?

But I'm not a monster.

Those spikes are there to help defend me against predators. I have a passion for ants and can consume a few thousand of the little creatures every day!

I absorb moisture through my skin and my feet.

I'm a **praying mantis**. I am an insect, with big, bulging eyes .

Can you see my strong front legs? I use them to catch and kill my prey.

But I'm not a monster.

Some people call me a dead leaf mantis, because I look like a dead leaf on a tree. This is so that animals can't spot me and eat me!

I'm a **Japanese spider crab**.

I have the longest leg-span of any underwater creature and I can grow so tall I could tower over a human.

But I'm not a monster.

I eat small fish, but I can also use my claws to open shellfish.

My main predator is the octopus.

I'm harmless to humans, but they should avoid my razor-sharp claws!

I'm a **hairy frog fish**. I'm covered in sharp spines that look like hair.

But I'm not a monster.

The spines help me hide in coral or seaweed, to protect me from my worst enemies — lizardfish and scorpionfish.

Smaller fish are my prey. Quicker than a blink, my mouth opens wide to a colossal size ... and in they go!

There are many other creatures that look rather odd, or frightening, or silly, but things aren't always what they seem.

We shouldn't judge them by what they look like.

Ransom Reading Stars Phonics Phase 5 titles

Neat and Clean
Stunt Star
Three Clues
The Royal Chopper
Flip Flap Fox
Little Phantom
Meet the Dolphins
Airship Rescue
Caves
The Floating Markets of Bangkok
Looking at the Stars
Canute's Flute
Mudlarking
The Clink Clank Clunk
Spot the Magnets
Planets are Spheres
Hunting for the Northern Lights
Mr White's Whiskers
The Cunning Plan
Living in the Best Homes
Camping Kit
Games We Can Play
The King's Cats
Luke and the Mule

Dazzling Water Sports
Who Needs Water?
Ships and Boats
Look at My Tail
Willow Saves the Day
The Scooter Contest
Wild Weather
Stone Soup
The Singing Chef
Celest and the Crystal Bracelet
Fantastic Frogs
Jogging into Space

Bridges
The Adventure of the Sunken Gold
Sir Jeff's Birthday Treat
Shipwrecks
The Magic Clog Dancer
Skipper Kipper and the Treasure Chest

Monkey Mischief
Let's Visit South Africa
Climbing
Getting to Gran's
A Messy Mystery
The Lady with the Lamp
Ten Shed Fred
Foolish Ostrich
Get Your Skates On!
Telephones
Going by Bus
Tweet, Tweet, Parp!
Fire
The Fire of London
The Elephant's Child
Bikes Then and Now
The Best Nest
Bears
A Very Special Musician

Foxes
Farmer Flo's Happy Cows
The Frog in the Well
The Biggest Carrot in the World
Magical Creatures
"We Are Not Monkeys!"
How Will You Get There?
The Nest Quest
Ella's Dragon
Flutter By, Butterfly!
The Princess and the Pea
Space Flight
Fantastic Feet!
Muscat: Our City, Our Home
A Monster under the Bed
Spider Girl
The Moon Race
Explorers Past and Present
Changes: Heating and Cooling
Hide and Peek
Volcanoes
The Rubbish Robot
Jake the Snake
"I'm Not a Monster!"

A full-colour A1 poster is available, showing all the books in the Reading Stars Phonics programme, together with details of what each book covers. Contact Ransom for a free copy.

"I'm Not a Monster!"

Letters and Sounds Phase 5
Draws on everything in Phase 5

Word count **505**

This book uses letters and sounds and common exception words that are found in Phases 2 to 5.

This book uses the following common exception words from Phase 5:
people, water, where, through, many, because, any, eyes

ISBN: 978-180047-644-8
www.ransom.co.uk

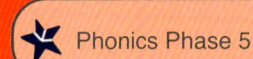
Phonics Phase 5

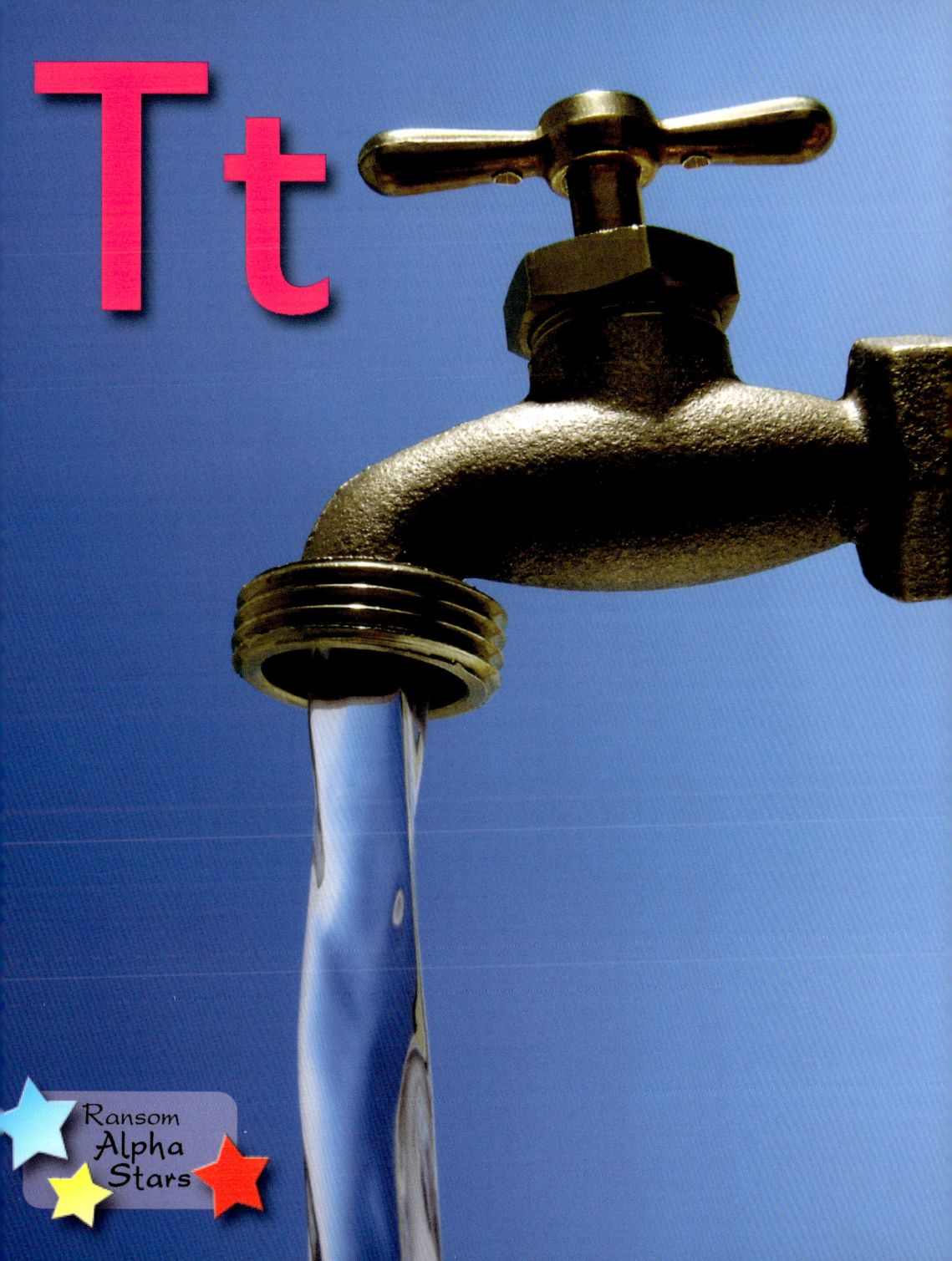

Ransom Alpha Stars
Tt
by Stephen Rickard

Published by Ransom Publishing Ltd.
Unit 7, Brocklands Farm, West Meon, Hampshire GU32 1JN, UK
www.ransom.co.uk

ISBN   978 178591 168 2
First published in 2016
Reprinted 2017, 2020

Copyright © 2016 Ransom Publishing Ltd.
Text copyright © 2016 Ransom Publishing Ltd.

A CIP catalogue record of this book is available from the British Library.

All rights reserved. No part of this publication may be reproduced, stored in a retrieval system, or transmitted, in any form or by any means, electronic, mechanical, photocopying, recording or otherwise, without the prior permission of the publishers.

The right of Stephen Rickard to be identified as the author of this Work has been asserted by him in accordance with sections 77 and 78 of the Copyright, Design and Patents Act 1988.